M

ALBORK

THE CASTLE OF THE TEUTONIC KNIGHTS

Words MARIUSZ MIERZWIŃSKI

Photographs MAREK ŻAK

Words and design
MARIUSZ MIERZWIŃSKI

Photographs
MAREK ŻAK

Reproductions
LECH OKOŃSKI

Proof-reading
MARIAN ARSZYŃSKI

Translated into English by:
TADEUSZ Z. WOLAŃSKI
© FAST, Gdańsk, Bażyńskiego 1

Typesetting:
FAST, Gdańsk

The Publisher wishes to thank the following: The Management of the Castle Museum in Malbork, the Management of the Gdańsk Library of the Polish Academy of Sciences, and the Management of the National Museum in Gdańsk for allowing the use of old views of Malbork in this book.

Bydgoszcz 1998

ISBN 83-903431-4-2

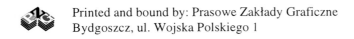 Printed and bound by: Prasowe Zakłady Graficzne
Bydgoszcz, ul. Wojska Polskiego 1

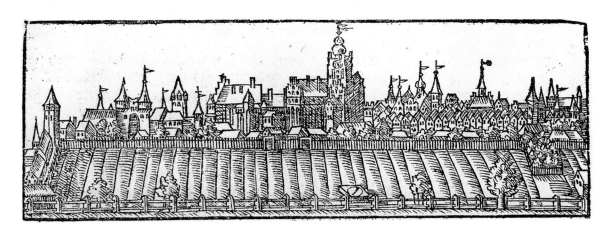

 mong the most characteristic elements of the low-lying landscape of north-east Poland, a particular place is occupied by fortified castles made out of red brick. Their pedigree goes back to the days of the distant Middle Ages, and most of them owe their existence to the construction activities of the Order of the Teutonic Knights. They have survived to this day in various states, some reasonably intact, while others are just picturesque ruins. All, however, exhibit a surprising perfection of building technique and a homogeneous style - features which make them an easily recognisable element of the Pomeranian landscape. The largest and the most impressive of them is undoubtedly the castle at Malbork, which from the beginning of the 14th century to the middle of the 15th century served as the capital of the Teutonic state in Prussia. The monumental, tripartite fort, imposingly situated on an elongated slope above the river, still arouses wonder at the skill of the old builders. Perhaps the wonder of today's visitors is coloured by an exaggerated dose of romanticism, perhaps we do not understand the full symbolism of this medieval monument, but each contact with it is a profound and unforgettable experience. The castle in Malbork is one of the greatest tourist attractions in northern

Poland. Nowadays we regard it primarily as an exceptionally valuable work of art - a monument of medieval architecture incorporating many wonderful structures which illustrate the development of Gothic vaulting and which present extremely valuable examples of the architectural art. Its carefully-planned use of space became a pattern followed by many later defensive structures. It is also a monument of the art of defence, showing in a clear and almost didactic way the development of defensive equipment from the 13th to the 19th centuries. This is an inexhaustible source of material for the scholar of the medieval and modern epochs. Finally, the castle is a monument of history, not only as the most representative symbol of the Teutonic Order, so hostile in its intentions towards the Polish state, but also as the residence of Polish kings and the seat of high levels of Polish administration, as well as one of the largest arsenals of the Republic under Polish government. It has now become a permanent part of the historic myth which is present in the consciousness of both Poles and Germans. But there are also elements here of the history of the inhabitants of Prussia, Lithuania, Samogitia, Sweden and France, not to mention representatives of many other nations coming here in the Middle Ages on Crusades against the pagans. It is difficult to over-estimate the importance of this site in the historic events taking place from the 14th to the 19th centuries.

The castle has now become an almost classic example of a monument illustrating the history of the development of European thinking about conservation and its practical application from the beginning of the 19th century to the present day. All of the conservation concepts realised in the castle over the last two hundred years by often great figures of art and science are preserved and protected these days in many parts of the castle complex. They are evidence of the care taken by many generations to preserve the cultural heritage by recreating with great determination the frequently destroyed parts of the castle.

In September 1994 the President of the Polish Republic issued a decree naming fifteen of the most important historic sites and complexes in our country as Monuments of History of special significance. Among them was of course Malbork Castle, which, in addition, was added to the world heritage list run by UNESCO. In this way the castle's high position among the most important monuments of the European cultural heritage was confirmed.

INTRODUCTION

he land once known as Prussia, with its western frontier on the River Vistula and its northern on the Baltic Sea and the River Niemen, was bordered to the east by lands occupied by Lithuanian tribes and to the south by Polish Mazovia. In the Middle Ages the land was covered by impenetrable forests full of extensive swamps and lakes. Its native inhabitants were pagan Prussians, related by blood to the Lithuanians and Latvians, a Baltic nation without a unified state, living by hunting, farming and limited animal husbandry, and occasionally by raiding. Organised in tribes, they lived in small rural settlements and occasional trading outposts scattered around the largely uninhabited areas of the country. The frequent raids by the Prussians against the lands of their neighbours meant that the Prussian-Mazovian border was not a peaceful one. It is not surprising therefore that Polish rulers from Mieszko I onwards were very interested in the lands stretching to the east of the lower River Vistula. Many times, however, the expeditions dispatched to the Baltic tribes met with failure, as did the attempts made by the Piast princes to defeat Prussia by force in the 12th century. The idea was born at this time to send for an order of knights, hardened by battle against the pagans in the Crusades to the Holy Land.

Summoned by Prince Konrad, the knights of the German House of the Hospital Order of the Blessed Virgin Mary from Jerusalem, known in Poland as the Knights of the Cross, arrived in Pomerania in around 1230. Their settlement in Chełmno County was supposed to guarantee the security of the borders of the Duchy of Mazovia against the attacks of the Prussian tribes, and to spread Christianity into the lands of Eastern Pomerania. The plans of the Polish princes to expand in this area were not without significance, particularly as they were to be realised with the support of the Order. The Knights, however, decided to take advantage of the ensuing opportunity to annex the Prussian lands for themselves and to establish their own state organisation there. Their clever diplomacy, conducted at the time by the outstanding politician and

Grand Master Hermann von Salza.

Print from: Ch. Hartknoch, Alt und Neues Preussen, Frankfurt 1684.

7

excellent organiser, Grand Master Hermann von Salza, led in 1234 to the acceptance from the hands of Pope Gregory IX of a bull allowing for the formation of such a state. When the Knights' autonomous intentions became apparent, it was too late for Poland, at the time undergoing partition, to oppose these intentions. The Order, as a military institution through and through, needed no more than 50 years to conquer Prussia. This was made possible above all thanks to the organisation of the armed forces from alien territory; the main base from which people and materials were drawn were the communities situated in the German lands. The glory of the armed mission conducted against the pagan Balts, together with the conscious cultivation of the ideal of the chivalric life at the end of the era of Crusades, brought the Teutonic knights considerable support among the knights of Western Europe among others.

In the conquered lands, the warrior-monks introduced a homogeneous, centralised system of administration divided into Commanderships. They conducted an intensive policy of colonisation based on settlers mainly from Germany and Poland. The guarantee of security for the Order was supposed to be a network of fortified castles built successively on the conquered lands. Initially these were wood and earthwork fortifications, using the local Prussian building technology and the locally available materials. Swiftly built during the military campaigns, they created the possibility of effective defence of the recently conquered lands. In time, along with the consolidation of the authority of the Order, there sprang up in their place enormous brick castles, serving not only a military purpose, but also acting among others as centres of monastic, administrative and economic life. The

Knights paid great attention to economic matters and this led in a relatively short time to the development of the country's economy. Soon, however, there appeared many unavoidable conflicts and disagreements within the Order, which was both a corporation of brothers devoted to the active propagation of the faith, and a feudal system administering a powerful state. This contradiction found its expression in the cultivation of the tradition of Western European chivalry and missionary battles against the pagans, along with simultaneous wars against Christian Poland and the bloody annexation of Gdańsk Pomerania. In this conflict, the idea of the state soon took precedence over the idea of the order, and the supremacy of political and material aims became prevalent in the whole history of the Teutonic Knights in Prussia. The conflict of the Order with Poland and Lithuania lasted for two centuries and left in the consciousness of the societies of both these countries a deeply-rooted feeling of grievance as a result of the activities of the Knights of the Cross. The memory of the most significant event of the conflict - the Polish and Lithuanian victory at the great Battle of Grunwald (Tannenberg) in 1410 - has for centuries lived as an important element of the glorious Polish historic tradition.

The Order of Teutonic Knights was the creation of a particular epoch, the time of the Crusades. By the 16th century, the Age of Reformation, it had already passed into history. Its state in Prussia was preserved in a vestigial form thanks to a restructuring in 1525 into a secular duchy and to becoming subservient to Poland. There remain to this day only the monuments of material and artistic culture, chief among which is the castle of Malbork.

THE BUILDING OF THE MONASTERY CASTLE IN THE 13TH CENTURY

he genesis of the building of Malbork Castle was most probably connected with the intention of the future expansion of the Order into Gdańsk Pomerania, as was the building at the same time of the castle in Gniew, on the left bank of the Vistula. The siting of the castle halfway between Gdańsk and Elbląg was also significant: on the crossroads of the old trade routes going east from Pomerania to the legendary port of Truso and further to Novgorod, and from the Sambia Peninsula to the south of Europe, to Italy (the ancient amber trail). The area chosen for the building of the castle had particularly good terrain - situated on a wide sweep of the River Nogat, the scarp fell gently away to the north while on the landward side there was a natural defence in the form of swamps. The river, apart from its natural defensive qualities, could be exploited as a means of communication and transport. The symbolic name of the town - Marienburg - was given in honour of the Order's patron, and from the beginning it seemed to endow the castle with a specific role.

Most probably the preparations for the building of the castle began in the first half of the 1270s, that is at the time when the head of the Order in Prussia was National Master Konrad von Thierberg the Elder. The fight against the second uprising of the people of Prussia was still continuing at that time and this forced the establishment of a temporary defensive camp, surrounded by a rampart and a moat, for the workers. Inside this camp there were provisional dwellings and building workshops. Significant deposits of clay in the region, particularly on the other side of the Nogat, meant that brickworks could be built in the immediate

vicinity of the building site. Great areas of forest were cleared, and large stones were collected and transported from the fields around for use in the foundations. Limestone quarries were also excavated. The organisation of such an enormous undertaking necessitated the calling in of a specialised building workshop, called in the Middle Ages a Bauhutte. Under the supervision of the Knights the work was carried out by master-builders most probably from Silesia, while the labour force mostly came from the local Prussian population. It is not known who the architect of this wonderful building was. This is in any case typical of the Middle Ages, when architects were simply called master-builders and no-one took any pains to preserve their names for posterity.

None of the building plans has survived from that period either, although it is known

The entrance gate to the High Castle, 13th century.

Print by B. Hellingrath, first quarter of the 20th century, in the Castle Museum Collection in Malbork.

that the basis for the work must have been some kind of documentation. In any case the design assumed the construction of a regular quadrilateral building surrounding an internal courtyard, in accordance with the model increasingly being favoured by the Order throughout Prussia.

The construction started therefore from the demarcation of a quadrilateral measuring 51.6 m. by 60.7 m. This was then surrounded by a defensive wall and encircled by a moat. The interior of the quadrilateral then began to be filled with buildings leaning against the aforementioned wall. The first to be built was the northern wing, in which were found the two most important buildings for the community of the order - the chapel and the chapter-house. In the Teutonic style they were located on the first floor, which served as the main storey. In the small interior between the chapel and the chapter-house were located the archives. The dormitory, or sleeping-quarters for the knights of the order, was temporarily sited on the ground floor under the chapel. The cellars had a provisional function - they were used as store-rooms.

Without interrupting their work the medieval master-builders began to erect the west wing and the tower, known as the Gdanisko, which extended beyond the quadrilateral in the direction of the Nogat. Access within the construction site was maintained by a two-winged, two-storey cloister supported from below on stone columns, with the roof made from wood. The other two sides of the quadrilateral - the east and south - were not enclosed; they were completed only by curtain walls topped with wooden constructions with loop-holes in the floor to enable attackers to be fired upon. The newly-built west wing took over the main accommodation and household functions. On the ground floor a kitchen and refectory, used for two meals per day, were constructed; the first floor was intended for living-quarters for the Commander and for his headquarters. Gdanisko, connected at the time with the main building of the castle by a porch with a draw-bridge, apart from serving a sanitary purpose (toilets), also served as the tower in the final line of defence.

Probably even before the above work was finished, somewhere around 1280, the Teutonic convent from Zantyra, a small town less than twenty kilometres to the south of Malbork, moved from its less favourable position to the new castle. It is not known exactly how many monastic knights lived at that time in the castle on the Nogat but it is known that their Commander was Heinrich von Wilnowe. Under his supervision the building of the first convent house, known from the 16th century as the High Castle, continued.

It is probable that the south wing, housing on the first floor two dark rooms intended as dormitories, was built by 1300. Above that it was planned to build a small convent room and store-rooms. Their planned shape underwent transformation as a result of the move of the headquarters of the Grand Masters to Malbork in 1309. Before 1300 there had already been built a representative entrance to the chapel in the north wing, the Golden Gate, belonging today to the most highly valued examples of architectural sculpture in Malbork. The deep vestibule formed in the thickness of the south wall of the chapel was covered with cross-rib vaulting, in whose keystone was depicted the figure of Christ in a mandorla. The portal itself was adorned with multi-form relief decoration, which in a symbolic way presented the subject of the Last Judgement and the parable of the wise and foolish virgins. The iconographical content was enriched by an apocalyptic thread, expressed in fantastic monsters woven into the floral decorations of the capitals and the

A wonderful view of Malbork.

Lithograph from the magazine: Przyjaciel Ludu, no. 30, 1839.

archivolt. The sculpted elements of the Golden Gate were made from terracotta and then covered with rich polychrome. Today only vestiges of the paintwork remain, but even they allow us to imagine the original effect.

Thanks to the gradual construction of successive sides of the quadrilateral, there was formed an inner courtyard similar in character to a monastic cloister. In the middle of it was bored a well almost twenty metres deep to ensure an independent water supply for the inhabitants in case of siege. The entrance into the courtyard was through the main gate, situated in the north-west corner of the fortress; defensive considerations caused the entrance to be constructed at an angle to the castle buildings. The entrance portal was made from granite blocks, while the sharply-pointed archivolt was decorated with a brick frieze with a three-leafed clover motif.

At the same time as the finishing touches were being put to the convent house, the Teutonic knights built along the north wall extensive approaches to the castle, intended for household stores. This was an area in the shape of a trapezium, surrounded on three sides by a defensive wall with towers in the corners and with several buildings located next to the perimeter walls. Only from the side of the convent house were the approaches free of walled fortifications.

In this shape in the year 1300 the castle in Malbork was no different from any of the other buildings of the Teutonic Order in Prussia. It was constructed in accordance with the predominant pattern of monastery-forts with a regular quadrilateral being built up inwards on all four sides around a central courtyard. Other castles built by the Teutonic knights in the Vistula basin at this time looked the same: Brandenburg (Pokarmin) and Lochstedt, as well as the previously-mentioned castle in Gniew, on the other side of the Vistula.

At the beginning of the 1280s there grew up a settlement near the castle, to which National Master Konrad von Thierberg the Younger gave the privilege of foundation. From that time there developed a thriving urban organism, but one which would remain throughout its history in the shadow of the massive castle next to it.

THE EXTENSION OF THE CASTLE
IN THE 14TH CENTURY

 he further fate of Malbork was affected by historic events in distant Palestine. In 1271 the Turks captured Montfort Castle, the main seat of the Teutonic Knights in the Middle East, then twenty years later the last Teutonic stronghold - Akkon. This signified the end of the Order's activities in the Holy Land. The headquarters of the Grand Master was temporarily transferred after 1291 to Venice, and the knights began to look around for another possibility of forming their own state, independent of secular power. They had some unfortunate experiences behind them already, as they had tried to exploit the Borsa lands which they had been given in Transylvania and to make them independent of the Hungarian state. In 1225, the Hungarian king Andrzej II saw through their plan and forcibly expelled them from Transylvania.

A significant event in the light of later happenings was the choice in 1291 of Konrad von Feuchtenberg as the Grand Master of the Order. As the National Master of Prussia and Livonia he had come to know the Baltic states very well. As Grand Master resident in Venice he had visited Malbork twice. Probably during his reign in 1295 the decision was taken to transfer the centre of Teutonic authority to Prussia. This transfer in fact took place some fifteen years later, after the Order had annexed Gdańsk Pomerania in 1308-1309. The addition of this land to the Teutonic state fundamentally changed the geopolitical situation of Malbork. From being one of the Commanders' castles on the western borders of Prussia, it now found itself virtually in the centre of the area under the control of the knights. In the middle of

September 1309 Grand Master Siegfried von Feuchtwangen moved his headquarters from Venice to Malbork.

The decision to locate the main residence of the highest authority of the Teutonic Order in Malbork Castle had a fundamental significance for the further construction history of the castle. The needs of the expanded administration of the Order, together with the representative functions of the court of the Grand Master, demanded an appropriate base and framework. From the first quarter of the 14th century there began a reconstruction of the present convent house together with a change of the original

A view, from the east, of the main tower, the Church of the Blessed Virgin Mary, and the Klesza Tower.

Illustration after a watercolour by J.C. Schultz, middle of the 19th century. From the Castle Museum Collection in Malbork .

plan for the use of this building. The castle had until that moment been a typical Commander's castle, but from about the middle of the 14th century it took on the form of a tripartite defensive structure and became one of the most powerful fortresses of medieval Europe.

As a result of the reconstruction, the internal building of the four wings of the High Castle took on its final shape and surrounded the quadrangle of the inner courtyard. To the curtain wall was added a fourth wing on the east side with a dormitory for the knights on the main floor and several floors of storage space above. This enabled the second floor of the south wing to stop being used as a storage space and to become a splendid complex of two rooms: a seven-pillared refectory and a convent house for resting after dinner.

The most significant building changes, however, took place in the oldest of the wings, the north wing, housing the chapter house and the chapel. The chapter house had always belonged to the most important rooms in each monastic community, being the place in which were discussed every day the most important matters concerning the community and where decisions were taken. Bearing in mind that Malbork was now the capital, and therefore was of great importance in the administration of the state, this particular chapter house had a very singular role to play. The interior, which up till then had been covered by simple cross vaulting supported on two pillars, was extended towards the chapel at the cost of the old archive room and the ceiling was greatly raised. The result was an impressive hall, whose monumental nature was enhanced by modern three-fold vaulting supported on three slender pillars. The most important element of the decor of the new chapter house was the gallery of Grand Masters, painted on shields on the walls above the ornamental backs of wooden stalls. The portraits of the most eminent Teutonic personages in this place were supposed to recall their virtues and to emphasise the endurance of the institution of the Order. This was undoubtedly one of the first examples of a conscious creation by the Teutonic Knights of the tradition of a monastic state in Prussia.

Around 1335 the biggest undertaking to date was started in the High Castle - the extension of the chapel in the north wing. The original small chapel took up one half of the wing and was housed in the compact quadrilateral of the convent house. In order to extend it, it was necessary to go beyond the confines of the quadrilateral. The east gable wall was therefore knocked down and the interior was extended by about 19 metres in an easterly direction, and the polygonal enclosure of the presbyterium was supported on the first line of defensive walls. The unicameral interior was covered by beautiful star vaulting, decorated by painting and illuminated by enlarged, sharply-pointed stained-glass windows. The completion date of the construction work - 1344 - is known from the consecration inscription preserved on the frieze below the windows.

The extensive vaulting was supported on uncommonly decorative slender pillars, whose most important element was the almost life-size figures of the apostles; cast from artificial stone, and richly polychromed, the figures stood on stone consoles under equally ornate canopies. On the lower part of the walls, separated from the vaulting by a powerfully delineated moulding, there was an interesting frieze in the form of blind arcades running around the whole of the interior. These arcades were filled with paintings depicting figures from the Old and the New Testaments. In the west wall there was situated a gallery porch with a particularly beautifully decorated ornamental wall opening leading to the

A view of the castle from the other side of the River Nogat.
Illustration by H. Ulbricht, 1907. From the Castle Museum Collection in Malbork.

interior of the church. The interior must have been equally richly decorated, but unfortunately not one example of medieval furnishing from this chapel has survived to this day.

An absolutely unique element of the architectural decoration was the statue of Mary and the Child, installed in about 1340 in an internal window alcove in the church. The colossal figure, over 8 metres in height, was cast in segments from artificial stone and covered in polychrome. The execution of such a large cast in situ, even in segments, would have been a considerable problem in the Middle Ages; only recently have Polish scientists been able to explain the complicated techniques involved in creating the statue. It seems that the creators of the statue were the same masters who created the sculpted decorations in the interior of the church.

In the second half of the 14th century the huge sculpture and the entire alcove were covered by a colourful mosaic. The creators of this original form of decoration were probably Venetian masters. The location of this statue, its supernatural size, as well as the atypical form of covering, indicate the enormous significance attached to this figure. Undoubtedly this was supposed to glorify Mary as the patron of the church and the town, but also the status of Malbork as a capital gave Mary and her statue the character of guardians of the whole Order and its state.

The extension of the presbyterium of the Church of the Blessed Virgin Mary beyond the mass of the quadrilateral of the High Castle led to the creation beneath it of new subterranean rooms. The Crypt Chapel of St

Anne was created here as the last resting-place of the Grand Masters of the Order. It was covered by star vaulting with richly polychromed ribs. On the east side was built a small altar alcove, while under the floor there were crypts for the tombs. Entrance to the interior was by way of two facing doors, one to the north, the other to the south. Both portals were wonderfully sculpted, similarly to the Golden Gate in the Church of the Blessed Virgin Mary. The decoration of the north portal consisted of three tympana with figurative decoration depicting scenes from the life of Mary: the Adoration of the Magi, the Assumption, and the Coronation of the Blessed Virgin Mary. The relief of the Coronation in the main tympanum was completed by the moral tale, known already from the Golden Gate, of the wise virgins, being led by an angel through the Gates of Heaven, and the foolish virgins, led by Satan into the jaws of the Leviathan. The south portal, leading to the cemetery of the knights of the Order, showed scenes associated with Christ: the Ascension, the history of the finding of the Holy Cross, and the Last Judgement. In addition, in the blind arcades beneath the area of the capitals, there were four large figures of apostles, cast in artificial stone. The Chapel of St Anne was completed in around 1340 during the reign of Grand Master Dietrich von Altenburg, incidentally the first to be buried there, in 1341. Today it would be futile to search for the traces of the eleven great dignitaries of the Order who were buried here. There are only three Gothic grave-stones left: those of Dietrich von Altenburg, Heinrich Dusemer and Heinrich von Plauen.

At the same time as the chapel and the new presbyterium of the church were being built, just next to them was erected a slender quadrilateral bell-tower. It was also supposed to serve as an observation point. Six storeys of the tower rose above the crown of the walls of the High Castle. The bottom four storeys were divided by ornamental arcade friezes. At the top of the tower there was an open balcony for the guard, protected by crenellations with raised corners. In this way appeared the highest point in the panorama of the castle.

The Great Refectory.

Illustration by F. Frick after a drawing by F. Gilly, 1799. From the Castle Museum Collection in Malbork.

All four wings of the High Castle were covered by high saddle roofs with steep slopes and with ceramic tiles of the monk-and-nun type. Both storeys of the cloister, allowing access around the interior of the High Castle, were clad in brick and given cross vaulting. Its main storey, opening out onto the inner courtyard with a row of sharply-pointed window openings filled with decorated tracery, was given a special decoration: both the vaulted roof and the shields were covered with rich polychrome. Today only a small fragment has been preserved of a larger painting probably depicting the hunting of a boar.

The greatest building activity took place in the area to the north of the High Castle, where up till then had been the Castle Approaches. The old household storage areas were transformed into a second monumental part of the castle, which was to fulfil a representative and administrative role. The area enclosed by the original defensive walls was extended, and fortifications were built to enclose an area of 1.5 hectares in the shape of a trapezium. Adjacent to the new defensive walls there appeared a three-winged construction around an inner courtyard. This was later called the Middle Castle and was open only on the side of the High Castle but separated from it by a deep moat. In keeping with the slope of the land, the area of the courtyard fell away gently to the north, which increased the feeling for people entering the castle from that side of the monumental nature of the High Castle filling their sight-lines.

On the east side a long brick building was erected as accommodation for the numerous Teutonic Knights arriving in the 14th century from all over Europe on Crusades against Lithuania and Samogitia. In order to avoid looking like a store-room, the facade of the building on the side of the courtyard was divided by sharply-pointed alcoves, on

the pattern of the west wall of the High Castle. In each alcove there appeared an uncommonly wide window filled with decorative tracery, through which anyone walking along the passage-way could observe the courtyard and the representative wing opposite. For the spiritual needs of the guests housed here the small Chapel of St Bartholomew was built at the southern end of the wing. The chapel extended a little beyond the mass of the building towards the west into the courtyard, from which entrance could be gained to the interior of the chapel through an ornate portal.

The north wing was divided into two parts by a massive gate-tower, which constituted the main entrance into the Middle Castle. In the eastern part, next to the guest rooms, there was created a row of representative, three-vaulted rooms intended for the living-quarters and headquarters of the Grand Commander. On the western side, where more storeys separated by horizontal beams were created, an infirmary or hospital was built. In today's understanding of a medieval hospital, this was rather a resting-place for the old and disabled knights. In the infirmary could be found large baths, a refectory with an ante-chamber and a small chapel in the basement, and living-rooms on the first floor. Both parts of the north wing had their own sanitary systems, located in the small corner towers extending out towards the north. These were linked to the main building by wooden passage-ways.

The west wing was mostly devoted to the needs of the Grand Master and his court. Here were to be found the greatest architectural masterpieces. The clearly visible influences of Western European architecture are proof of the thriving contacts that the Order had with almost the whole of Europe. These contacts were undoubtedly made easier by the network of Teutonic communities, mostly in Germany and

France. The wealthy treasury of Malbork, together with the ambitions of the Grand Masters to match the splendour of Western European courts, had a wonderful effect. Around the middle of the 14th century, in the middle of the west wing, the biggest room in the Order's secular architecture, and one of the most beautiful interiors in Europe, was created: the Great Refectory. Wonderful tri-partite vaulting, with the three parts more highly developed than in the chapter-house, was supported on three, very slender octagonal granite pillars. The architecture, complemented by wall paintings, was decidedly dominant in this spacious interior, while sculpture found a humble place for itself on the three capitals and on the bases of the pillars, as well as the consoles and keystones of the vaulting. Of the once rich polychrome, all that is left today is a fragment of the painting of the Coronation of the Blessed Virgin Mary on the shield above the entrance. The Great Refectory was primarily used for the banquets held for the knights of the Order and their guests from various countries of Europe. On the north side there was the kitchen with its great hearth where all the dishes were prepared. Next to the kitchen were some small rooms, probably a store-room and the cook's quarters.

Throughout the whole of the 14th century work continued on the southern part of the west wing, near the bridge leading to the High Castle. Here was constructed the Palace of the Grand Masters, a construction whose architectural class matched that of the greatest European residences of the late Middle Ages. The construction of the first residence intended for the highest authority of the Order was commenced in this place after the decision was taken to transfer the main headquarters to Malbork, that is after 1309. The successors of Siegfried von Feuchtwangen had at their disposal a small rectangular building on the site of the future Palace. Work on creating a more impressive residence began after the completion of the extension of the High Castle, probably around 1345, during the reign of Grand Master Heinrich Dusemer. At that time was constructed a rectangular building extending beyond the line of the west wing towards the River Nogat.

In 1382 Grand Master Konrad Zollner von Rotenstein decided to rebuild the existing building so that it matched the residences of European rulers. Work at this time went on mostly on the west wing, where representative interiors were to be created. This enterprise was continued with panache by Konrad von Jungingen. During his reign, at the end of the 14th century, the reconstruction of the eastern part of the Palace, carried out under the supervision of master-builder Mikołaj Fellenstein, brought to an end the medieval history of the construction of this wonderful building. He built an impressive residential tower extending beyond the line of the west wing in the direction of the river, referring architecturally to Burgundian and English patterns. The logically planned interiors, clearly divided into a private part on the northern side, and the representative part on the south and west, were richly painted at the beginning of the 15th century, as befitted the most important seat of one of the richest orders of medieval knights. The polychroming in the interiors on the main floor was the work of the studio of Master Piotr, the Malbork court painter. Most of the vaulting was adorned with floral decoration, whose abundant red and green foliage formed a kind of floral canopy over the spacious interiors. The walls were treated monochromatically in red, or else motifs of figures and ornaments, including heraldic devices, were introduced.

In the Palace's Chapel of St Catherine one can still see the painted figures of the apostles Peter and Paul, almost life-size,

The Palace of the Grand Masters in winter.

Lithograph by A. Rahnke after a drawing by J. Hoorn, 1831. From the Castle Museum Collection in Malbork.

while in the small bedroom of the Grand Masters there are very beautiful figures of four holy virgins: Dorothy, Margaret, Catherine and Barbara. An interesting group of paintings is found in the gallery of the Grand Masters, on the shields of the Winter Refectory, second only to a similar gallery in the chapter-house of the High Castle. Two interiors in the part of the Palace extending towards the River Nogat - the Summer and Winter Refectories - were covered by wonderful late Gothic radial vaulting supported on one pillar. They belong to the greatest architectural achievements in all the lands of the old Teutonic state.

The reconstruction of the existing Castle Approaches into the representative Middle Castle meant that there was a need for a new household storage area, on a greater scale than before. It was decided to site it on the area next to the Middle Castle on the northern side. In the first half of the 14th century it was surrounded by a defensive wall. On the eastern side, the one most vulnerable in the case of a siege, the wall was strengthened by eight massive towers and by the main entrance gate onto the area

of the Castle Approaches, the Snycerska (Wood-carvers') Gate. The buildings were sited along the eastern defensive line and had above all a military character - armouries, coach-houses, arms workshops. The dominant building was the huge mass of the Karwan, the biggest Teutonic arsenal. Along the wall overlooking the River Nogat were built granaries and store-houses for goods transported by river. Their substantial area indicates the amount of trade carried out by the knights, primarily in grain, timber and amber. Inside the defensive walls were built stables, barns, sheds, malt-houses, fuel-stores, and servants' quarters. On the western side was built, in stages, a long complex of household buildings. At the southern end of these was built the Church of St Lawrence for the servants and next to this, sharing the gable wall, was the hospital for the German mercenaries.

Level with the High Castle, within the riverside fortifications, a double-entry gate was built, flanked by two short, round towers. This gave access to a wooden bridge across the river. The bridge and the gate were built by Grand Master Dietrich von

Altenburg, who was well-known for his construction activities in Malbork. It may have been at the same time that the slender Maślankowa (Buttermilk) Tower, also known as the Modra (Blue) or Lichnowska Tower, was built, climbing above the fortifications of the Castle Approaches in the north-west corner. Its marvellous proportions make it one of the most picturesque fragments of this part of the castle.

The siege of the castle by the armies of the king of Poland, Władysław Jagiełło, after the Battle of Grunwald in 1410, clearly brought home to the Teutonic Knights the danger posed to the walls of the castle by artillery. In order to further strengthen the defence of the fortress, and at the same time to put as great a distance as possible between the residential and representative parts of the castle and the artillery positions of the enemy, in the first half of the 15th century another defensive line was built on the eastern and northern sides. A massive wall was placed along the external edge of the so-called von Plauen rampart and strengthened by the addition of several low, semi-cylindrical towers capable of housing artillery pieces. This undertaking, started during the reign of Grand Master Konrad von Erlichshausen, was the last building work to be completed by the knights in Malbork.

THE CASTLE UNDER POLISH RULE 1456-1772

he growing discontent of the subjects towards the ever more severe hand of the ruling Teutonic Order led in 1440 to the establishment in Kwidzyn of the Prussian Union. This was a confederation of the nobles and the towns of Eastern Pomerania formed to guarantee internal security and defence against the injustice of the Orders administrators. The sharp conflict between the Union and the Teutonic authorities led in February 1454 to the outbreak of an armed anti-Teutonic rebellion in the whole of Prussia. At the same time the envoys of the Prussian states issued an act stating that Prussia owed allegiance to the King of Poland as the rightful ruler of the Pomeranian lands, once annexed by the Teutonic Order from the Crown.

King Kazimierz Jagiellończyk, the son of the victor of the Battle of Grunwald, did not refuse their request and issued an act in March 1454 incorporating all the Prussian lands into the Kingdom of Poland. This was the direct cause of the eruption of the Thirteen-Year War between Poland and the Teutonic Order, which led to the recapture by Poland of Gdańsk Pomerania and Chełmno County, as well as the occupation of the Żuławy region together with parts of Warmia and Pomezania. From then on these lands became known as Royal Prussia. The capital of the state, Malbork, also shared their fate.

During these battles the Order - going through a period of deep internal crisis and serious financial troubles - was forced to cede to its mercenary forces several castles, including Malbork, as surety against payments due. The Teutonic Order on several occasions failed to meet deadlines for the payment of these due moneys, which led the Czech mercenaries to turn to the King of Poland with a proposition for the sale of the castle to the king for the then enormous sum of 190 thousand florins. Kazimierz Jagiellończyk accepted this proposition and on 8 June 1457 made his triumphal entry into the castle, abandoned in haste the previous day by Grand Master Ludwig von Erlichshausen. From that time onwards the further destiny of the castle has been linked with the history of the Polish state.

Malbork became the seat of high offices of Polish administration: the starost (district elder), the treasurer of the Prussian lands and the voivode. The latter soon transferred his seat to Sztum, but still styled himself the Voivode of Malbork. The highest authority was in the hands of the starost, who was nominated by the king. Direct supervision of the castle, including the maintenance and supplying of the fort, was carried out by the burgrave, who answered to the starost. On 1510 King Zygmunt the Old created from his possessions in the Żuławy region the Malbork Stewardship and called into being a new post to administer it - the Steward of Malbork. The Steward also resided in the castle. The proceeds from the Stewardship were transferred directly to the King's Treasury.

The new residents partly changed the designation of some of the castle buildings. The greatest changes affected the use of the High Castle, whose interiors were used as household storage areas, above all for the storage of food, as well as for accommodation for the leaders of the castle staff. Naturally the Church of the Blessed Virgin Mary retained its spiritual role, but

St Nicholas's Gate in the Castle Approaches.
Illustration by B. Hellingrath from the first quarter of the 20th century. From the Castle Museum Collection in Malbork.

from this time it served only as a branch of the town's parish church.

The Middle Castle kept its original function as a residential and administrative area. In the north and east wing lived the officials mentioned earlier. The Great Refectory stayed as a dining-hall, where the starost met his military staff during meals. Sometimes the king would host great banquets here during his visits to Pomerania, for example during the knighting of the 22-year-old Bogusław, later the Duke of Pomerania, by Kazimierz Jagiellończyk in 1476. A royal residence was prepared in the old Palace of the Grand Masters for the Polish monarch. To this end the southern and eastern parts of the main floor were used. In the most representative room of the Palace - the Summer Refectory - took place conventions of the states of Royal Prussia and meetings between their representatives and the king's commissioners.

Also most of the buildings in the Castle Approaches kept their original functions, above all for military and household use. There were however certain changes: for example, in one of the segments of the row of buildings on the western side there used to be, during the reign of King Zygmunt III Waza, a mint. In time the Approaches became a more and more independent centre of economic activity, developed by the numerous craftsmen who settled there.

Most of the information on the subject of the economic management of the castle during the Polish period comes from the descriptions included in the audits of the Malbork Stewardship. The audits were carried out in the 16th, 17th and 18th centuries by royal commissioners. The first one took place in 1565, while subsequent ones occurred as needed, generally when the Steward was changed. On the basis of these accounts one can deduce that the defensive nature of the fortress was still maintained in the 17th century and that the old defensive measures, such as drawbridges, gates, embrasures and loop-holes, were still in use. From the pages of old inventories one can form an opinion about the wealth of the castle in terms of military materials, which were mostly stored in the post-Teutonic armoury in the Approaches (the Karwan), at that time a very significant armoury for the Republic of Poland. A considerable part of the weapons, particularly the fire-arms (harquebuses), was housed in individual towers and turrets, known at that time as guards.

Thanks to the huge grain stores, the timber stores, the well-stocked arsenal and the powder-mills, Malbork was a great supply base in case of war on the Baltic Sea. Many times the kings of Poland used this base, for example during Stefan Batory's expedition in 1577 against the rebellious city of Gdańsk, or during the Polish-Swedish dispute over Livonia at the beginning of the 17th century. Throughout the 16th and 17th centuries a permanent Polish military force of some 200 people was stationed in the castle. At times of danger the number of soldiers was increased according to the needs of the situation and the available resources. Direct command of the forces was in the hands of the starost.

It is not possible to forget the role of Malbork in King Zygmunt August's plans to build a powerful fleet on the Baltic Sea. From 1568 the Maritime Commission, otherwise the first Polish Admiralty commanding the Royal Navy, had its headquarters in the castle. Its office accommodation was most probably in the east wing of the Middle Castle, where the guests of the Order used to be housed. The Commission's activities were financed, among others, from the proceeds from the Malbork stewardship.

From the moment that Kazimierz Jagiellończyk took over the castle, it was a long time before the Gothic style of construction changed. The first reconstruction took place in the second half of the 16th century, as a result of the changing needs of the castles new inhabitants. At that time the treasurer, and at the same time the steward, Jan Kostka, erected, with the king's permission, a wooden residential manor-house on the southern side of the courtyard in the Middle Castle. In this way a fourth wing was formed in this part of the castle, and this was consolidated a few years later by the joining of the court to the royal residence in the Palace on the western side, and to the east wing, by a covered passage-way.

The manor-house has not survived to our day, and nothing is known about the decoration of the interior. On the basis of other parts of the castle, it can be stated with some certainty that there must have been a great deal of painted decoration. Some twenty years ago it was still possible to see the remains from the Polish period of the painted ceiling in the long hall above the chapter-house. Another example of Renaissance painting, executed in the monochromatic technique en grisaille, was to be found adorning the north wall of the Chapel of St Bartholomew.

In the middle of the 1580s the main tower, topped until then with crenellations, received its first dome. Treasurer Jan Dulski built a Renaissance coping in the form of a pinnacle with a copula and spire, which in an elegant way emphasised the mass of the castle tower. The same iconographical sources from which we know the shape of the Renaissance dome show the appearance of large clock faces on the external walls of the tower underneath the dome. This is in accordance with a mention in written sources of the existence in the 16th century of a clock and bells on the top of the tower.

The adaptation of the main storey of the Palace into a temporary residence for the kings of Poland did not initially entail any greater constructional changes. There was in fact no need for them. In the interiors there appeared only one new colourful element - tiled stoves which slowly began to replace the archaic medieval system of underfloor heating. It was not until around 1600 that the reconstruction of the eastern part of the Palace chapel took place. On the orders of King Zygmunt III Waza a representative staircase was built, allowing access from the courtyard to the royal apartments on the first floor. From the room adjoining the old chapel an angled corridor was built through to the ante-chamber and on to the Winter Refectory, whose interior in turn was divided into two levels by the addition of a new wooden ceiling and into smaller rooms by the addition of partition walls.

In 1626 the Swedes entered Prussia and started another war with Poland. After fierce battles for Malbork, the Swedish king, Gustavus Adolphus, took the castle in July.

It was only the Truce of Sztumska Wieś in 1635 that returned Malbork to Poland. The battles for the castle and the several year long occupation by the Swedes led to a serious devastation of the site. Many of the roofs were damaged by the artillery attacks; the breaches led to further destruction caused by the actions of the weather. The worst fate befell the constructions around the Castle Approaches, many of whose fragments simply ceased to exist, for example the entire central part of the row of household buildings on the western side. These wartime effects were exacerbated by a fire in 1644, which destroyed most of the roofs in the High Castle, the top storey of the Gdanisko Tower and the Renaissance

Portrait of Gerard Denhoff against the background of Malbork Castle.

Copperplate engraving by W. Hondius, 1643. From the Collection of the Gdańsk Library of the Polish Academy of Sciences.

Illustrissimus et Excellentissimus Dñus Geerhardus Comes à Dœnhoff, Palatinus Pomerelliæ, Terrarum Prussiæ Thesaurarius, Capit: Marizburgens: SKarzeviens: Bernens: Lucinens: Stilinens: Regiæ Oeconomiæ Mariæburgensis Administrator, etc

Gulliclmus Hondius Hago Bataves ad Vivum Deliniavit et æri incidit.

dome on the main tower.

Luckily for the ruined castle, it found itself in the hands of one of the most outstanding royal administrators in the whole of the Polish period - Gerard Denhoff. Born in Malbork, this diplomat and soldier was the trusted advisor of, and one of the closest collaborators with, King Władysław IV. In the 1640s, until his death in December 1648, he accumulated several of the highest positions in Prussia: Voivode of Pomerania, Treasurer of Royal Prussia, Starost and Steward of Malbork. His great achievement was the restoration of a large part of the Teutonic fortress. In the High Castle he replaced the roofs on the north and west wings, and repaired the upper parts of the walls of the Gdanisko Tower and the pent-roofs above the cloisters around the courtyard. The new rafters were considerably lower than the original ones, which to a great extent changed the Gothic silhouette of the oldest part of the castle complex. In the Middle Castle he restored the Chapel of St Bartholomew in the east wing, which had been devastated by the Swedish army. When the work was finished the chapel was reconsecrated as the Chapel of St Wojciech (Adalbert). In the Approaches he rebuilt the seriously damaged household buildings beyond the Church of St Lawrence, the village elders' granary beside the River Nogat, and the old Teutonic armoury against the eastern defensive wall, which he turned into a brewery. Many rooms were repainted and refitted with new wooden fixtures, windows, floors and tiled stoves. Realising how important it was to ensure constant professional supervision of such a large complex of buildings, King Jan Kazimierz, in 1649, soon after Denhoff's death, appointed a permanent master-builder for the castle. This was Tomasz Hertmański, who moved into the old guard-house by the draw-bridge leading to the High Castle. It can generally be stated

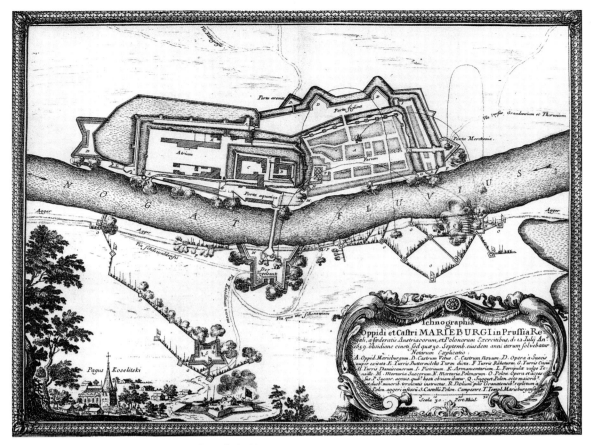

Plan of Malbork at the time of the Swedish Wars.

Illustration from the print by S. Puffendorf, De rebus a Carolo Gustavo Sveciae rege gestis..., Nuremberg 1696.

that the decade around the middle of the 17th century until the second Swedish invasion was probably the best period for the castle in all its time under Polish rule.

The stormy second half of the 17th century did not permit the completion of the reconstruction of the damaged fortress. The second Swedish-Polish War of 1665-1660, known traditionally as The Deluge, brought further devastation to the castle buildings. At this time began the slow decline of the Malbork arsenal. Building works were restricted by the war-depleted state of the royal treasury. The crisis was deepened by the numerous passages of soldiers from Saxony and Russia, which affected Malbork

at the end of the 17th century and which continued throughout the first half of the 18th century.

The only substantial building works at this time were carried out by the Jesuits, who had settled in the castle as early as 1618 but who only started intensive activity after the second Swedish-Polish War. In the second half of the 17th century they took over the castle church and restored its interior. At the end of the century and during the first half of the 18th they paid for the baroque decoration of the church. This consisted of four altars (the main altar and three side ones), the pulpit, the organ and the benches. Around the middle of the 18th century the

Jesuits erected a several-storey brick-built college between the church and the east wing of the Middle Castle. For over a hundred years it was a significant element of the panorama of the castle until it was demolished at the end of the 19th century as part of the Gothic restoration of the castle.

In the second half of the 17th century and throughout the 18th century the castle slowly lost its military significance, and the defensive equipment, through lack of conservation, was gradually reduced. The walls and the towers slowly crumbled, which was not helped by the waters of the Nogat overflowing their banks. The Republic's attention at this time was focused on the Turkish borders, from where the greatest danger was perceived. Gradually into the Approaches encroached haphazard domestic dwellings, surrounding ever more closely the High Castle and the Middle Castle. The builders of the new houses used the old defensive walls to lean their houses against, so that in the middle of the 18th century it was no longer possible to recognise the structure of the old fortifications.

The last important works in the castle during the Polish period of rule were the rebuilding of the roofs above the south and east wings of the High Castle, which had been destroyed by fire in 1644, the rebuilding of the Gothic cloisters surrounding the courtyard into baroque ones, and the erection by the Starost Michał Ernest Rexin in 1756 of a new baroque dome on the main tower. This Starost also renovated the rooms used by the Malbork administrators in the north and east wings of the Middle Castle, and rebuilt the western part of the Chapel of St Anne in the High Castle, incorporating therein a new crypt.

Thus ended the first long period of the existence of this building, during which it underwent changes, but not radical ones. Throughout the whole of this period the castle was permanently occupied by people who had a definite concept of its exploitation, which was in a certain sense a continuation of its original function.

THE PRUSSIAN PERIOD AND THE TIME
OF RESTORATION 1772-1945.

 he years 1772-1804 are among the most tragic in the history of Malbork Castle. The occupation of this historic fortress by the armies of Frederick II as a result of the First Partition of Poland in 1772 signified the end of this fortress's importance. The castle was not prepared for the conditions of life in the 18th century and it was treated by the above all practical Prussian administrators as a place serving various casual ends, including as a source of building materials.

The conversion of the historic buildings, initially into barracks (1773-1774), then into military store-rooms (1801-1804), led to radical reconstruction and irreversible devastation. Almost all the Gothic vaulting was torn out of the High Castle and it was replaced with wooden store-room ceilings. The new storeys created in this way were illuminated by rows of newly-built rectangular windows. From the town side, another entrance into the castle was created, allowing for direct access into the courtyard thanks to a wide passage-way ripped through the south wing.

In the Middle Castle the entrance gate and the upper part of the Kurza Noga (Hen's Leg) Tower, once used as the sanitary section of the Infirmary, were demolished. Into the representative interior of the Palace the occupiers introduced a two-storey construction and new partition walls to help the hastily introduced manufacture of cotton and for dwellings for the weavers. The turning of the Great Refectory into a drill-ground for the army was a death-sentence passed on the rich interiors and decorations of this wonderful room. In the Approaches they dismantled the Gate of

St Lawrence and the Wołowa (Beef) Tower, located among the fortifications on the northern side. Enormous losses were incurred with the destruction of historic doors, windows, floors, stoves, as well as other architectural features and valuable examples of old furnishings. The height of the utilitarianism of the Prussian administrators was the plan to demolish the whole castle and to use the materials thus acquired to build great store-houses. This enterprise, planned by the secret government official David Gilly, never came to fruition, because of the high costs involved.

At the end of the 18th century the Romantic element began to dominate in European culture, rejecting the pragmatism of the Age of Enlightenment and bringing a fascination with the Middle Ages. Old buildings became significant as memorials to the past, and respect for them no longer needed to have a utilitarian basis. Also in Malbork Castle spiritual values were noticed - both artistic and historical. Great interest was aroused in the castle in Germany by the publication in 1799 of an album containing graphic illustrations of views of the castle. Three young Berlin artists, Friedrich Gilly, Friedrich Frick and Friedrich Rabe, were entranced by the marvellous architecture and by the beauty of the detail and they presented to the world the values of this historic building, which was threatened by further devastation.

Under the pressure of public opinion, a government decision was taken in 1804 ordering the cessation of devastation and placing the building under a protection order, as a monument of earlier architecture. In this way the castle in Malbork became one of the first historic monuments in

The north wing of the Middle Castle after the Romantic restoration around the middle of the 19th century.

Woodcut from M. Rosenheyn's book: Die Marienburg, Leipzig 1858.

Europe to be placed under a conservation order. The early work undertaken here also paved the way for other old buildings to be similarly protected.

It was in 1817 that the first, so-called Romantic, reconstruction began, intending to restore the castle to the splendour, according to the idealised picture of the authors of the project, that it had previously had. The great advocate of this restoration and its long-standing patron was the President of Prussia, Theodor von Schon, who dreamed of turning the castle into the Pantheon of the Prussian Province, comparable even with Westminster in London. Work concentrated almost exclusively at this time on the Middle Castle, and in particular on the Palace of the Grand Masters. In the High Castle, only the main tower received a new top in place of the demolished baroque dome, removed because of its poor technical condition. After only ten years of intensive restoration activity, the representative rooms

of the main floor of the Palace had regained their former glory. Particular attention was paid here to filling all the windows with stained glass, depicting, among other things, figurative scenes from the life of the Order.

Next in line were two wings of the Middle Castle - the west and the north - which were adorned with battlements, basically because of a mistaken idea about Gothic architecture. Similarly unfounded was the erection of a triangular summit on the Great Commandership, which seemed to the then supervisor of construction, Gersdorff, an essential element of the elevation of the Middle Castle. Today all these bold effects of the Romantic way of looking at the architecture of the castle can be seen only in old pictures and in photographs in the archives. Successive years brought an evolution in the way of thinking about the methods of conserving monuments and, as a result, the elements from the early 19th century which were regarded as unjustified were removed from the structure of the building. The few surviving examples of the work of the Romantic restorers are today solicitously being looked after; no small importance in this matter is attached to the fact that one of the people taking part in these restorations was the outstanding German architect Karl Friedrich Schinkl.

The effects of the first restoration of the castle had as early as the middle of the 19th century come in for criticism at the hands of the first conservator of monuments in Pomerania, Ferdinand von Quast. This versatile pupil of Schinkl's was an advocate of preceding all work associated with historic monuments with archaeological and architectural research. He also initiated the initial measuring and exploring work, as well as the excavating in the oldest part of the complex, in the area of the High Castle. In 1851 his work, entitled Schloss Marienburg, appeared in print. In this work he proposed, among other things, a new and unusually accurate chronology of the history of the construction work at Malbork. From this time there slowly began to develop the first conception of the total reconstruction of the castle, only to be realised at the end of the 19th century by Konrad Steinbrecht.

In contrast to the Romantic vision of the castle from the period of its first restoration, the building and conservation work at the end of the 19th and the beginning of the 20th centuries conducted by the architect Konrad Steinbrecht were preceded by detailed research in the archives, studies of the architecture, and excavation. The results of these studies of the historical material formed a scientific base for the recreation of the elevation of the building and of the interior construction, the shape of the rooms and the architectural detail. Any lack of necessary data on the site was made up for by knowledge of other Teutonic castles. While recreating the fixtures and fittings use was made of existing examples of preserved medieval furnishings in the castles and monasteries of Western Europe. A huge amount of documentation, not to be found anywhere else, was gathered, which means that we now have a rare opportunity to analyse precisely the process of reconstruction.

The work started in 1882 and within fifteen years Steinbrecht completed the Gothic restoration of the oldest part of the complex, the High Castle, whereas work on the Middle Castle went on until 1923. As a result a work was created which is in effect an illustration of a conception of what the castle looked like at the height of the Teutonic Order's glory at the end of the

A romantic view of the castle from the other side of the River Nogat in the first half of the 19th century. *Engraving in steel after D. Quaglio, about 1830. From the Castle Museum Collection in Malbork.*

Middle Ages. Steinbrecht realised his own vision of an ideal Teutonic castle, based on the principle of unity of style, and removing any elements from the construction from periods later than the medieval period, including the Polish, the Friedrich and the Romantic additions. The reconstructor did not merely rebuild just the Gothic form of the castle. He strove to create within it an illusion of life, filling the recreated interiors with furnishings from the epoch in which the knights lived in the castle. These elements included original items, as well as carefully made copies. During the restoration work there was formed in the castle one of Europe's richest collections of architectural elements, coming both from Malbork and from other historical monuments in Pomerania. This collection, gathered in several lapidaria, became a valuable source of materials for comparative studies, and was used during conservation work, including that which took place after the catastrophic destruction of the last war.

The political conditions surrounding the reconstruction of the castle at the end of the 19th century are a very important matter.

The Romantic era, together with Gothic architecture and the castle, also discovered its creators - the Teutonic Order, which had either existed in the memory in Prussia in a negative way, or had been entirely forgotten. Its history was now incorporated into the general history of Germany and upon this was built throughout the 19th century the German tradition of presence in the East. Malbork, as the capital of the Teutonic state, took on a special significance in this ideology.

At the end of the 19th century the historic fortress was given a new role - it was to be one of the residences of the Kaiser of a united Germany. Theodor von Schon's dream from the first half of the century of a Prussian Pantheon, a place where all free citizens could meet, was transformed into a government building, a place of state ceremonies with a decidedly anti-Polish character. The Teutonic castle had been restored to its former glory so that it could fulfil the function of a historical monument, reminding Germans about their ancient rights to the fatherland.

THE CASTLE AFTER 1945

ndoubtedly none of the German conservators rebuilding the medieval walls with such devotion in the 19th and early 20th centuries could have supposed that the castle would have to serve its old purpose as a fortress once again. Strongly fortified towards the end of the Second World War, Malbork for two months stood up to the besieging forces of the Red Army. The German defenders, gradually losing their positions in the town, retreated to the castle, where the last act of the drama took place. The capture of the town on the River Nogat in March 1945 was bought at a terrible price: the catastrophic destruction of the ancient parts of the Old Town and the demolition of many priceless parts of the castle.

As a result of the long-lasting artillery attacks, nearly all of the buildings in the Castle Approaches lay in ruins: the Karwan, or the old Teutonic armoury and coach-house, the House of the Under--Starost, the Ludwisarnia (Bell-foundry), the row of household buildings beyond the Church of St Lawrence, and the New Gate. Out of over a dozen towers in the external line of ramparts only the round Buttermilk Tower in the north-east corner of the Approaches and the two towers of the Bridge Gate over the Nogat survived. The main parts of the complex - the High and Middle Castles - offered from the east a dramatic sight: shattered outer walls, damaged roofs and gaping holes instead of windows. An enormous breach in the Church of the Blessed Virgin Mary and the Chapel of St Anne meant almost total destruction of the priceless complex of these two holy places and of the high bell-tower, from the 14th century the highest point in the panorama of the castle. Until the war, it was these parts, together with the Palace of the Grand Masters, which had contained the greatest percentage of medieval elements. Together with the polygonal presbyterium of the church was destroyed the mosaic figure of the Madonna, which broke into thousands of little pieces. Also destroyed was the south-east top of the High Castle with part of the vaulting of the convent house, the House of the Bell-ringer on the north terrace, and a large fragment of the east elevation of the Klesza Tower, which was hammered by shells and whose vaulting was destroyed on two storeys. A huge breach in the east wing of the Middle Castle showed the place where there had previously been a representative room with

The Church of the Blessed Virgin Mary in the High Castle from the south-eastern side; after the devastation of 1945.

Photograph: The Archives of the Castle Museum in Malbork.

The Castle from the east after the end of the war.

Photograph: The Archives of the Castle Museum in Malbork.

vaulting supported on six pillars. The destruction did not spare the Palace of the Grand Masters, where a shell shattered two pillars of the eastern elevation, piercing the wall and the 19th century vaulting of the corner room.

Thousands of cubic metres of rubble covered the courtyards, moats and interiors, burying many historical architectural elements and valuable exhibits from the pre-war museum. Among the piles of rubble and glass were fragments of smashed furniture, burnt sculptures and torn and soaked prints from the collections of the Gdańsk and Pelplin Libraries, deposited in the castle during the war to protect them from the advancing front. A considerable part of these priceless books had been used by the defenders of the castle to barricade the windows in the absence of sandbags.

The remnants of wooden roof-rafters, hanging from the holes in the walls, threatened at any moment to fall down. The damaged roofs, the breaches in the walls and the shattered windows allowed the weather to do its worst to the rest of the surviving interiors and the furnishings. The curator of Gdańsk voivodeship at the time, Professor Jan Borowski, estimated that the castle had been 50% destroyed during the war.

Nowadays only a few remaining ruined buildings in the Approaches bear the scars of those days. The only proof of the scale of the destruction done to the two main parts - the High and Middle Castles - exists in photographs in the archives. The restoration work has taken the thirty-five years of the existence of the Castle Museum and this great work has restored the castle once again to its former glory. The painstaking conservation is slowly removing the last traces of the wartime damage, and expresses the attitude of the current guardians of the castle to this wonderful monument as a work of art in the universal sense.

Between 1945 and 1950 the management of the complex was in the hands of the Polish Army Museum in Warszawa, which organised one of its branches here. The first work began to secure the area and to clear it. The most important achievement at the time was to repair most of the damaged roof coverings, which was done despite the understandable difficulties with finding materials and contractors. This allowed the monument to survive until the time came to begin professional and planned conservation work. During the 1950s the castle was managed by the Polish Tourist and Excursion Society. The work undertaken at this time - clearing and minor repairs - had an ad hoc nature and was connected with the ever-growing tourist trade. Work at the

castle took on a more decided tempo at the end of the 1950s when the Social Committee for the Reconstruction of the Castle was formed by local cultural activists. This Committee called into being the institution of the museum to look after the monument.

The turning point in the post-war history of the castle was the great fire, which, on the night of 7/8 September 1959, destroyed the roof over the north and west wings of the Middle Castle. This was a powerful shock, which made everyone realise the shortcomings of the existing protection of this valuable site. From 1 January 1961 the Castle Museum took over the management of the whole historic complex. The Museum had been established primarily to restore and conserve the site and to manage and maintain appropriately the Gothic fortress on the River Nogat. The beginning was particularly difficult because of the complex nature of the conservation work. There was no complete scientific documentation, the pre-war archives of the Reconstruction

The reconstruction of the east wing of the Middle Castle, 1968.

Photograph:
The Archives of the Castle
Museum in Malbork.

Board were scattered all over the place, and there were significant gaps in the old collections of architectural details and elements. All of this meant that it was difficult to make the right choice about the sequence of work, the best method of conservation of the walls, and the correct shape of the damaged fragments of the walls. As the work progressed the appropriate scientific documentation began to be gathered, and slowly a group of people began to form, better and better prepared from the professional point of view, and completely devoted to the whole enterprise. Most of the building and conservation work was carried out by the specialist company The Conservation of Monuments Studio, whose branch in Gdańsk created a separate section in Malbork to meet the particular needs of the castle itself.

The post-war reconstruction of the castle complex in Malbork, although it has not yet finished, constitutes a lasting and important chapter in the most recent history of Polish conservation of monuments. We treat it at the same time as a continuation of the complex building activities in this wonderful place, clearly written into its elevations and interiors through the multi-coloured bricks, their irregular arrangements and various textures. The effect of the efforts of many generations of conservators can be appreciated just by strolling around the walls of the castle.

Two hundred years have passed from the moment when the young architect Friedrich Gilly from Berlin drew a series of views of Malbork Castle, something which is now regarded as the first example of conservationist interest in this Teutonic fortress. On this important anniversary, on a great boulder in the courtyard of the Middle Castle, a commemorative plaque was dedicated to all the conservators who for the last 200 years had devoted at least part of their lives, knowledge and hearts to this magnificent building. To those who despite all the odds made an effort to ensure that Malbork Castle would survive to serve future generations.

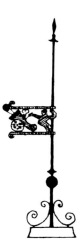

The south-eastern part of the Middle Castle after the clearing of the rubble in the 1950s. In the background there is a surviving fragment of the walls of the Church of the Blessed Virgin Mary with its two high windows.

Photograph: The Archives of the Castle Museum in Malbork.

The High Castle from the south-eastern side after the end of the war. >>

Photograph: W. Hodakowski.

A SELECTION OF THE MOST RECENT PUBLICATIONS:

Arszyński, M., *Budownictwo warowne zakonu krzyżackiego w Prusach (1230-1454)*. Toruń 1995.

Biskup M., Labuda G., *Dzieje zakonu krzyżackiego w Prusach. Gospodarka - społeczeństwo - państwo - ideologia*. Gdańsk 1986.

Borchert F., *Burgenland Preussen. Die Wehrbauten des Deutschen Ordens und ihre Geschichte*. Munich-Vienna 1987.

Chodyński A.A., *Zamek Malborski w obrazach i kartografii*. Warszawa 1988.

Haftka M., *Malbork. Album - przewodnik*. Warszawa 1988.

Haftka M., Mierzwiński M., *Malbork. Zamek krzyżacki*. Warszawa - Munich 1992.

Jakubowska B., *Złota Brama w Malborku. Apokaliptyczne bestiarium w rzeźbie średniowiecznej*. Malbork 1989.

Kilarski M. *Mozaikowa figura malborskiej Madonny*. Malbork 1993.

Mamuszka F., *Marienburg - Elbing - Frauenburg*. Dulmen 1995.

Mierzwiński M., *Zamek w Malborku*. Warszawa 1993.

Mierzwiński M., *Malbork*. Wrocław 1995.

Okulicz-Kozaryn Ł., *Życie codzienne Prusów i Jaćwięgów w wiekach średnich (IX-XIII w.)*. Warszawa 1983.

Skibiński Sz., *Kaplica na Zamku Wysokim w Malborku*. Poznań 1982.

800 Jahre Deutscher Orden (Exhibition catalogue from the Germanisches Nationalmuseum in Nuremberg). Gutersloh/Munich 1990.

GRAND MASTERS OF THE TEUTONIC ORDER

1. Hospital Brotherhood

Residence: Akkon (until c. 1230?)

Sibrand 1190

Gerard 1192

Heinrich 1193/1194

Ulrich 1195

Heinrich (Walpot?) 1196

2. Order of Teutonic Knights

Heinrich Walpot 1198-1200

Otto von Kerpen 1200-1208

Heinrich von Tunna, called Bart 1208-1209

Hermann von Salza 1209-1239

Residence: Montfort (Starkenberg) (c.1230?-1271)

Konrad von Thuringen 1239-1240

Gerhard von Malberg 1244-1249

Heinrich von Hohenlohe 1244-1249

Gunther von Wullersleben 1249-1252

Poppo von Osterna 1252-1256

Anno von Sangershausen 1256-1273

Residence: Akkon (1271-1291)

Hartmann von Heldrungen 1273-1282

Burchard von Schwanden 1282-1290

Residence: Venice (1291-1309)

Konrad von Feuchtwangen 1291-1296

Gottfried von Hohenlohe 1297-1303

Siegfried von Feuchtwangen 1303-1311

Residence: Malbork (Marienburg) (1309-1457)

Karl Beffart von Trier 1311-1324

Werner von Orseln 1324-1330

Luther von Braunschweig 1331-1335

Dietrich von Altenburg 1335-1341

Ludolf Konig 1342-1345

Heinrich Dusemer 1345-1351

Winrich von Kniprode 1352-1382

Konrad Zollner von Rotenstein 1382-1390

Konrad von Wallenrode 1391-1393

Konrad von Jungingen 1393-1407

Ulrich von Jungingen 1407-1410

Heinrich von Plauen 1410-1413

Michael Kuchmeister von Sternberg 1414-1422

Paul von Rusdorf 1422-1441

Konrad von Erlichshausen 1441-1449

Residence: Królewiec (Konigsberg) (1457-1525)

Ludwig von Erlichshausen 1450-1467

Heinrich Reuss von Plauen 1467-1470

Heinrich Reffle von Richtenberg 1470-1477

Martin Truchsess von Wetzhausen 1477-1489

Johann von Tiefen 1489-1497

Friedrich von Sachsen 1498-1510

Albrecht von Brandenburg-Ansbach 1511-1525

Residence: Mergentheim (1525-1809)

Walter von Cronberg 1527-1543

Wolfgang Schutzbar called Milchling 1543-1566

Georg Hund von Wenckheim 1566-1572

Heinrich von Bobenhausen 1572-1590/95

Maximilian von Osterreich 1590/95-1618

Karl von Osterreich 1619-1624

Johann Eustach von Westernach 1625-1627

Johann Kaspar von Stadion 1627-1641

Leopold Wilhelm von Osterreich 1641-1662

Karl Joseph von Osterreich 1662-1664

Johann Kaspar von Ampringen 1664-1684

Ludwig Anton von Pfalz-Neuburg 1684-1694

Franz Ludwig von Pfalz-Neuburg 1694-1732

Clemens August von Bayern 1732-1761

Karl Alexander von Lothringen 1761-1780

Maximilian Franz von Osterreich 1780-1801

Karl Ludwig von Osterreich 1801-1804

Residence: Vienna (from 1809)
Anton Victor von Osterreich 1804-1835

Maximilian Joseph von Osterreich-Este 1835-1863

Wilhelm von Osterreich 1863-1894

Eugen von Osterreich 1894-1923

3. Priestly Order
Norbert Klein 1923-1933

Paul Heider 1933-1936

Robert Schalzky 1936-1948

Marian Tumler 1948-1970

Ildefons Pauler 1970-1988

Arnold Wieland 1988-

The Grand Master in the uniform of the Order
Illustration from P.H.Helyot's Ausfuehrliche Geschichte aller geistlichen und weltlichen Kloster - und Ritterorden. Leipzig 1754. The Gdańsk Library of the Polish Academy of Sciences.

HERMANN von SALZA

The fourth Grand Master of the Order, he served in this role from 1209 to 1239. He was born around 1179 and came from a ministerial family in Thuringia. He was the real creator of the Order and one of its greatest Masters; he transformed a small corporation into a strong organisation of a political and military character. He was blessed with uncommon political talents and several times went on diplomatic missions for Frederick II. He made the first attempt to create a Teutonic state in eastern Europe, in Transylvania in 1211-1225, but this ended in total failure. Replying positively to the challenge of the Mazovian Duke Konrad he became the founder of the Teutonic state in Prussia. He died in 1239 in Salerno and was buried in the Order's chapel in Barletta in south-west Italy.

SIEGFRIED von FEUCHTWANGEN

The fifteenth Grand Master of the Order, he held the post from 1303 to 1311. He came from Franconia from the same family as the thirteenth Grand Master, Konrad von Feuchtwangen. Little is known of his earlier activity, and his name only appears in documents at the end of the 13th century: in 1298 he was a Master of the German lands, and a year later he was Commander in Vienna. He became Grand Master after the abdication of his predecessor, Gottfried von Hohenlohe, at a time of internal dispute in the Order. During his reign, in 1308, the Teutonic Knights brutally annexed Gdańsk Pomerania and became Poland's greatest enemy. In September 1309, Siegfried transferred the headquarters of the Order from Venice to Malbork. He died in 1311, in Malbork, and was buried in the cathedral in Chełmża.

KARL BEFFART von TRIER

The sixteenth Grand Master of the Order, he fulfilled this function from 1311 to 1324. Born around 1265, he came from an old patrician family in Treviro. He was regarded as one of the best educated knights in the Order. In the 1290s he was a Commander in the French and German communities, and in 1304 he accompanied Grand Master Siegfried von Feuchtwangen in Venice as a Grand Commander. He favoured reform in the Order, but his attempts met with resistance (among other things, he created the office of manciple, the only brothers who could engage in trade). A great struggle in the hierarchy of the Order meant that he had to leave Prussia in 1317. In 1318, at the general meeting of the Chapter, he was restored to his title of Grand Master but did not return to Prussia. He retired to Treviro where he died and was buried in the Church of St Catherine.

WERNER von ORSELN

The seventeenth Grand Master of the Order, from 1324 to 1330. He was born around 1280 and probably came from Hesse. He was the protege of, and a close collaborator with, Grand Master Karl from Treviro. Between 1312 and 1313 he was the Commander of Ragneta, an important frontier fort against Lithuania. From 1314 to 1324 he was a Grand Commander. He became Grand Master in Malbork in July 1324. By attacking Kuyavia in 1327 he started a war with Poland. He was instrumental in colonising and cultivating large parts of Prussia. During his reign the personal chancellery of the Grand Master, known as the small chancellery, was set up. He was also active in the reconstruction of Malbork, in particular the fortifications. He was murdered in November 1330 by Brother Endorf of the Order, when he was coming out of the chapel in the High Castle in Malbork.

DIETRICH von ALTENBURG

The nineteenth Grand Master of the Order, from 1335 to 1341. He came from Thuringia. Between 1320 and 1324 Commander of Ragneta, then of Bałga (1326-1331). From 1331 he was a Grand Marshal and conducted raids against Poland, conquering Kuyavia for the Order. An energetic and cruel man, he was the main accused before a Papal Tribunal, for his part in the crimes committed in the 1331 raids. As Grand Master he was very active in building and reconstruction work in the Order's castles. In Malbork his work was particularly important as he began the reconstruction of the Church of the Blessed Virgin Mary and the building of the main tower. He also commissioned the mosaic figure of the Madonna, finished the Chapel of St Anne and built the first permanent bridge over the Nogat, and the Bridge Gate. He fell ill and died in October 1341 in Toruń, where he had come to negotiate with Poland. He was the first Grand Master to be buried in the Chapel of St Anne in Malbork; his original grave-stone can still be seen there to this day.

HEINRICH DUSEMER

The twenty-first Grand Master of the Order, he held the post from 1345 to 1351. He was born around 1280 and probably came from Franconia. As Commander of Ragneta in 1329 he began his military education with war against the Lithuanians. Five years later he was Commander of Brandenburg (Pokarmin) and Grand Marshal from 1335 to 1339. After the abdication of Grand Master Ludolf Konig in 1345 he became Governor of Prussia, and a few months later, in December, he was chosen Grand Master. He was one of the Order's greatest colonisers, particularly in southern Prussia. It was he who probably began the construction of the representative Palace of the Grand Masters in Malbork Castle and completed the Great Refectory in the Middle Castle. In 1351, because of illness, he resigned from office and settled in Bratiano, where he died two years later. He was buried in the Chapel of St Anne in Malbork, where his grave-stone can still be seen to this day.

WINRICH von KNIPRODE

The twenty-second Grand Master, from 1352 to 1382. Born around 1310 in Lorraine. From 1338 to 1341 Commander of Gdańsk, then in 1342 of Bałga. Grand Marshal from 1342 to 1346 during the reign of Grand Master Ludolf Konig. Heinrich Dusemer named him Grand Commander in 1346. After Dusemer resigned he became Grand Master and was the longest serving head of the Order in the whole Medieval period. His reign is regarded as the period of the Teutonic state's greatest power. This was also the time when the secular spirit held decided sway in the Order. In 1365, as the first Master, he hosted the King of Poland, Kazimierz the Great, in Malbork. He continued the building of the Palace of the Grand Masters. During his reign the town walls of Malbork were built. He died in 1382 in Malbork and was buried in the Chapel of St Anne.

ULRICH von JUNGINGEN

The twenty-sixth Grand Master of the Order, from 1407 to 1410. He was born around 1360 in Swabia and was the younger brother of his predecessor as Grand Master, Konrad von Jungingen. Between 1391 and 1392 he held the post of Grand Master's Companion (to Konrad von Wallenrode, a figure known to 19th century literary scholars). From 1396 to 1404 he was Commander of Bałga, then from 1404 Grand Marshal. As Grand Master he strove for war with Poland and eventually declared it in 1409. During the so-called Great War between the Order and Poland, the decisive battle was on 15 July 1410 at Grunwald (Tannenberg), one of the greatest battles in medieval Europe. The Order's might was broken, and Ulrich von Jungingen's body was sent by King Władysław Jagiełło from the battlefield to Malbork, where it was buried in the Chapel of St Anne.

HEINRICH von PLAUEN

The twenty-seventh Grand Master, from 1410 to 1413. He was born around 1370 in Thuringia. From 1399 to 1402 he was Domestic Commander in Gdańsk, then Commander of Nieszawa (1402-1407) and Świecie (1407-1410). After the Battle of Grunwald (Tannenberg) he defended Malbork Castle against the besieging Polish armies and was consequently chosen Grand Master later in 1410. He reigned briefly and only with the help of bloody repression. He was constantly seeking disputes with Poland to have revenge for Grunwald. He was overthrown by a coup led by dignitaries of the Order and was imprisoned together with his brother, the Commander of Gdańsk. He spent the rest of his life in the castle in Lochstedt, where he died in 1429. He was buried in the Chapel of St Anne in Malbork, where his grave-stone can still be seen to this day.

MICHAEL KUCHMEISTER von STERNBERG

The twenty-eighth Grand Master, he held this post from 1414 to 1422. He was born around 1370 and probably came from Silesia. From 1402 to 1405 he was Grand Manciple in Królewiec (Konigsberg). During one of the Order's attacks on Poland at the end of 1410 he was taken prisoner at the Battle of Koronowo and was imprisoned until summer 1411. On his return to Prussia, Heinrich von Plauen nominated him Grand Marshal. As Grand Master he advocated peace. To strengthen Malbork he continued the building work started by his predecessor on the fortifications on the eastern side. At this time the master-builder Mikołaj Fellenstein erected the so-called Nowa (New) Gate. Not being able to prevent war with Poland, and losing the trust of his fellow brothers, he resigned as Grand Master. After his abdication in March 1422 he retired to Gniew, and then Gdańsk, where he died in 1423.

LUDWIG von ERLICHSHAUSEN

The thirty-first Grand Master, he held the post from 1450 to 1467. He was born around 1410 in Swabia and was the nephew of his predecessor, Konrad von Erlichshausen. From 1436 to 1440 he was the Companion to the Grand Master, Paul von Rusdorf, then Commander of Pomeranian Kowalewo (1442-1447) and of Gniew (1446-1450). He was a limited and impetuous man, and expended most of his energy on fighting the Prussian states and on seeking opportunities to attack the Prussian Union. Throughout almost all his reign the Order was engaged in a long-lasting war with Poland called the Thirteen-Year War (1454-1466), as a result of which the Order was forced to give Gdańsk Pomerania and Chełmno County to Poland, as well as losing Warmia, the Żuławy region and part of Pomezania, including Malbork. In 1457 Ludwig von Erlichshausen was forced to abandon Malbork and transfer the capital of the Order to Królewiec (Konigsberg), where he died in 1467.

ALBRECHT von BRANDENBURG-ANSBACH

The thirty-seventh Grand Master of the Order and the last in Prussia, he held the post from 1511 to 1525. In Poland he was known as Albrecht Hohenzollern. He was born in 1490, the son of the Margrave Friedrich von Brandenburg-Ansbach and Zofia, the daughter of the Polish king, Kazimierz Jagiellończyk. From the time he took over the post of Grand Master, he planned to declare war on Poland and he eventually did so in 1520. The war ended a year later and was the last war between Poland and the Teutonic Order. In 1525 Albrecht secularised Prussia and paid homage to the Polish king, Zygmunt the Old, as the prince of a secular feudal state. This signified the end of the monastic state in Prussia. Albrecht was known for supporting artistic works and it is thanks to his cultural policy that a university was founded in Królewiec (Konigsberg). He died in 1568 in Tapiewo.

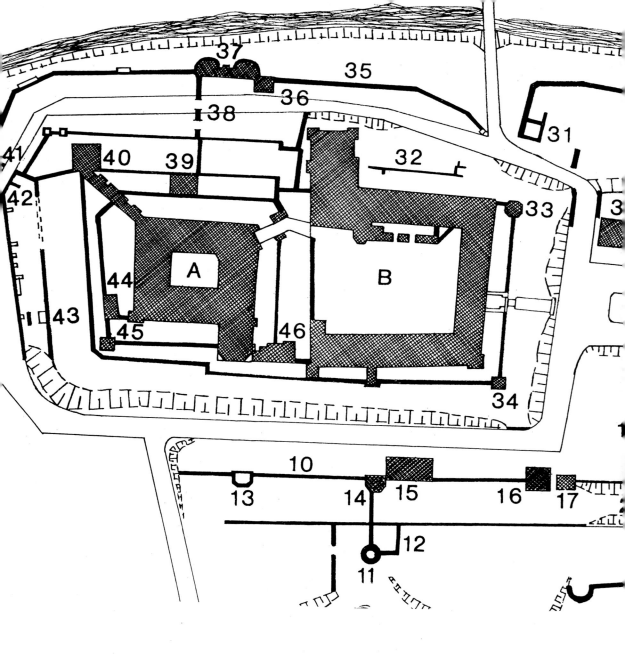

KEY:

A - HIGH CASTLE
B - MIDDLE CASTLE
C - CASTLE APPROACHES

1. Mill-race canal
2. Castle moats
3. Swedish earth-work (1656-1660)
4. Northern defensive wall of the Approaches
5. The so-called von Plauen Rampart
6. Szarysz Tower
7. Kominki (Chimney) Tower
8. Maślankowa (Buttermilk) Tower (a.k.a. Lichnowska)
9. Kęsa Tower

10. Main defensive line of the Approaches
11. Nowa (New) Tower
12. Nowa (New) Gate
13. Łupinowa Tower
14. Nad Piekarnią (Bakery) Tower
15. Armoury
16. Snycerska (Wood-carvers') Tower
17. Wójtowska (Village Elders') Tower (together with the Snycerska Tower formed the Snycerska Gate)
18. Museum Ticket Office
19. Karwan (armoury and coach-house)
20. Karwan manager's house
21. Prochowa (Powder) Tower
22. Trójścienna (Three-sided) Tower

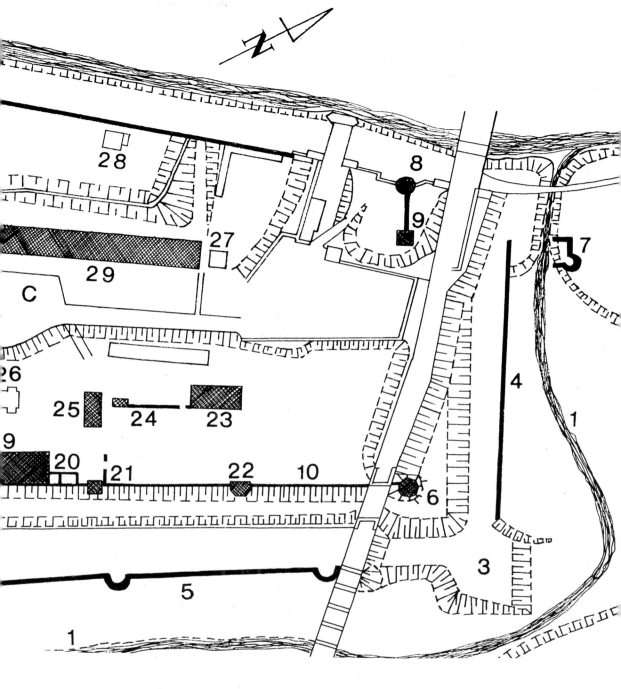

ILLUSTRATIONS

Northern elevation of the Middle Castle as seen from the Castle Approaches.

An autumnal view of the wooden bridge leading to the Middle Castle.

The entrance to the Middle Castle with the road leading to the courtyard.

Bas-relief above the entrance gate to the Middle Castle depicting the Mother of God - copy of a relief from one of the churches in Riga.

Fragment of the northern elevation of the Middle Castle with the ornamental top of the Infirmary and the Kurza Noga (Hen's Leg) Tower.

The Church of the Blessed Virgin Mary and the main tower in the High Castle, seen from the east.

The High Castle from the south-east.

Fragment of the eastern elevation of the High Castle with the presbyterium of the Church of the Blessed Virgin Mary, the Klesza Tower and the Bell-ringers House.

The Klesza Tower and the Gdanisko Tower in the Middle Castle, seen from Starościńska St.

Fragment of the eastern elevation of the castle, seen from the Approaches.

The fortifications of the Approaches from the east.

The northern end of the former Nowa (New) St in the Approaches with the Snycerska (Wood-carvers') Tower and the top of the old armoury (Karwan) in the distance.

The Bridge Towers seen from the river-bank.

The Bridge Towers in the middle of the fortifications on the banks of the Nogat on the western side.

A romantic view of the Palace of the Grand Masters. Painting by D. Quaglio, 1934. From the National Museum Collection in Gdańsk.

The Palace of the Grand Masters from the south-western side.

The High Vestibule in the Palace, leading to the representative rooms.

The Summer Refectory in the Palace of the Grand Masters - the most representative interior of the castle.

The south-western top of the High Castle.

The mass of the High Castle seen from the Palace of the Grand Masters.

Old ivy climbing the western wall of the High Castle.

The portal above the door on the west wall of the High Castle, from 1773.

The head of Grand Master Winrich von Kniprode.

Statues of Grand Masters of the Teutonic Order in the courtyard of the Middle Castle in front of the Palace; 19th century.

Bas-relief on the well in the Middle Castle, depicting Christ at James's wife's well.

Sculpture depicting Christ in the Garden of Gethsemane, beginning of the 15th century.

Linden tree in the courtyard of the Middle Castle.

The western side of the courtyard in the Middle Castle with the buildings in front of the Great Refectory and the Palace Chapel above them. On the left is the entrance to the bridge leading to the High Castle.

The well in front of the Great Refectory in the Middle Castle; building from the beginning of the 20th century.

Entrance porch to the north wing of the Middle Castle.

Bas-relief with the figure of a knight - copy of a medieval relief from the gate of the Teutonic castle in Bierzgłowo.

The entrance to the High Castle with the drawbridge.

The entrance to the High Castle with the guard-tower, seen from the Middle Castle.

A view from the drawbridge in the High Castle looking east; at the end of the deep moat is the high Klesza Tower.

A narrow gate leading to the courtyard of the High Castle.

The portal of the entrance gate to the High Castle, end of the 13th century.

The top of the well in the High Castle with a figure of a pelican feeding its young with its own blood.

The well in the courtyard of the High Castle, decoration from the late 19th century.

A view from the courtyard of the cloister near the west wing of the High Castle.

Granite pillars supporting the western side of the cloisters in the High Castle.

The cloister next to the oldest, northern, wing of the High Castle.

A knight on the capital of a column in the open-work of a window in the northern cloister.

Fragment of the sculpted decoration on the Złota (Golden) Gate with an image of a hybrid.

The main entrance to the castle church - the Złota (Golden) Gate, late 13th century.

The interior of the dining-room in the convent in the High Castle.

A room in the convent, once used for resting after dinner.

Wall-painting above the entrance to the Chapter-house in the High Castle, depicting the Madonna on the Throne. By Herman Schaper, late 19th century.

The main altar from Tękit, showing the Coronation of the Blessed Virgin Mary, 1504. From the Castle Museum Collection in Malbork.

Figure of an apostle from the Church of the Blessed Virgin Mary in the High Castle, c. 1340.

Stained-glass windows in the Chapter-house.